Ask the Ancients

Ask the Ancients

Astonishing Advice
for Daily Dilemmas

By
Sylvia Gray

Bolchazy-Carducci Publishers, Inc.
Mundelein, Illinois USA

Editor: Laurel Draper
Design & Layout: Adam Phillip Velez
Illustrations: Lydia Koller

Ask the Ancients
Astonishing Advice for Daily Dilemmas

Sylvia Gray

Bolchazy-Carducci Publishers, Inc.
1570 Baskin Road
Mundelein, Illinois 60060
www.bolchazy.com

Printed in the United States of America
2014
by United Graphics

ISBN 978-0-86516-818-3

Library of Congress Cataloging-in-Publication Data

Gray, Sylvia, author.
  Ask the ancients : astonishing advice for daily dilemmas / by Sylvia Gray.
    pages cm
  Includes bibliographical references and index.
  ISBN 978-0-86516-818-3 (pbk. : alk. paper) 1. Rome--Social life and customs. I. Title.
  DG90.G739 2013
  937'.63--dc23

                                                                                      2013039860

Contents

Lifestyles

Human Relations

Sociopolitical Issues

Government

Morals and Ethics

Metaphysical

Ultimate Questions

Acknowledgments

Thanks to Dr. Joseph B. Scholten for introducing the classical world to me.

Thanks to my former husband for confessing that *even he* thought these entries were interesting.

Thanks to the book club, "The Common Reader," for reading, commenting on, and encouraging this endeavor.

Thanks to my friends Shelley Baker-Gard and Susan Mosedale, among many others, for their supportive belief in this project.

Thanks to my husband, Viktors Berstis, for his love and confidence in me at all times.

Introduction and Explanation

When I enrolled in a classical history course and began reading the first assignment—it was Livy's *Early History of Rome*—I was amazed that I had never been introduced to him before. Livy was a fascinating storyteller. I loved his voice—he philosophized, he moralized, he complained, he eulogized. The inherent interest in these primitive tales certainly rivaled the charm of Bible stories I had grown up with.

I began reading other ancient authors and found that I couldn't get enough. I read Plutarch, Cicero, Suetonius, Seneca, Herodotus, Thucydides, and Homer, to name a few. I read more than was assigned for my courses. I determined to read everything extant from antiquity (a bigger undertaking than I ever imagined). I was constantly surprised by the universal aspects of human experience that shone through.

I could not contain my discoveries. So as not to overly bore my own friends, I began teaching history. I also began writing an *Ask the Ancients* column for a local paper, and I now offer you these collected columns.

This book offers only a sampling of the wisdom and foibles of these authors, who offer answers to many burning questions our modern world still asks. Their opinions are easily accessible, if you only know where to find them. Let me preface their advice with a few comments of my own.

These tidbits *are* representative—but only of the wide variety of possibilities from antiquity. I could have selected a different source and thereby presented a different viewpoint for any number of questions. Note one small example: Socrates believes in reincarnation and

Lucretius believes that when we die, our matter changes form and that's it. (Compare entries #8 and #51.)

These also offer only a taste of any given author's full persona. In some cases more complexities arise when the writer is read in entirety. Again, Plato's Theory of Forms briefly presented in entry #51 is a prime example. But, I would claim, I offer a representative introductory sip for a reader who desires to imbibe further.

Insightful as these writers often prove to be, in some cases they are not particularly politically correct, especially by current American standards. They have however been dead and gone for fifteen hundred years or more and there is no way they will be corrected now. If we don't care for their advice, we can maintain our own opinions, and I for one do not mind throwing in my own two bits. You'll be able to tell the difference.

Women writers are rather sparse here—simply because 99 percent (I'm estimating) of the extant literature from antiquity was written by men. Of course, as a woman, I will help make up for that lack.

I chose not to draw from other world traditions. One could, certainly. But I have remained within the Western classical tradition, which is profound and varied enough in its own way.

The dating scheme corresponds to the dated BC/AD. BCE stands for "Before the Common Era," and CE stands for "Common Era." Traditionalist though I am, I now bow before the new common usage.

Career and Workplace

-1-
Attaining Consensus

How can my committee reach a unified consensus?

– Decisionally Split

The second century CE historian Tacitus describes a unique and oddly sane method that the Germanic peoples used to arrive at agreements. Not that Tacitus had observed it or used it himself—but he did have a reluctant admiration for certain practices of these "barbarians," as he considered them. I'll bet it would work great, and wouldn't be half as boring as some committee meetings I've sat in, either.

The Germans would choose a feast or celebration for the occasion and would include drinking alcohol as part of the festivities.

> At no other time, they think, is the soul more open to sincere and broad-minded thoughts. They are without craft or cunning, and in the freedom of revelry expose their heart's secrets, so that every mind is frankly bare....

No decision was reached until the second stage:

> On the next day the matter is reconsidered, and account is taken of both discussions. So they debate when they are incapable of pretense, but make the decision when they cannot make a mistake.

Clearly, this is a process that includes both the irrational and the rational—and in the proper order. I'd say give it a try.

One caution: Tacitus does remark that during certain all-day/all-night drinking bouts accompanying the celebrations, quarrels were sometimes settled by wounding or killing. Try to avoid this.

You may read Tacitus's fascinating descriptions of this and many other curious Germanic customs in his Germania.

-2-
Climbing the Ladder

What is the most effective way to move up the career ladder?

– Motivated Climber

L et us ask Theophrastus, a prominent student of Aristotle who was later head of the Peripatetic school in the third century BCE, for his recommendations for advancing your career. This popular lecturer describes personality types, most of them not very flattering, in his book *Characters*. He suggests, in answer to your question, that "flattery is . . . a sort of converse that is dishonorable, but at the same time profitable, to him that flatters."

Here are some of the ploys that you may find useful: mention to your superior that other people talk favorably about him and give specific examples that make him look good. When he talks, silence others around him to get their attention. If his jokes are bad, laugh anyway. Be concerned for his comfort—check to see if he is too cold or too hot. Comment that his hair is still dark compared to many of his cohorts. Remark on his beautiful house, his well-landscaped yard (what Theophrastus actually mentions is well-tended fields), and his portraits. Be the first to praise the wine at a dinner party. Bring presents for his children.

Never mind that Theophrastus calls it "dishonorable"—he also calls it effective. If you imitate this lifestyle, you will experience great success in your career!

These suggestions were taken from "The Flatterer," only one of many types described in Theophrastus's CHARACTERS. *You may also read descriptions of other flaws, including cowardice, garrulity, nastiness, officiousness, stupidity, and tactlessness. You will undoubtedly recognize someone you know!*

-3-

Personal Hygiene in the Workplace

**Should I tactfully mention to my coworker that
his personal hygiene needs improvement?**

– Odoriferously Offended

While some may consider the question trivial, a situation of this sort can permeate the soul. In essence, one must choose whether to endure personal discomfort on a sensory level or risk interpersonal awkwardness on a social level.

The great and conscientious Roman emperor Marcus Aurelius (second century CE) deemed the question of enough import to include it in his *Meditations*. No doubt he had had plenty of experience with the problem, living as he did for so long in the army camps on the edge of civilization. He treats the issue as a matter of maintaining one's psychological balance:

> Are you angry with a person whose armpits stink? Are you angry with him whose breath smells bad? What good will your anger do you? He has that sort of mouth and armpits: . . . that kind of smell comes from those things. . . . You have reason: by your reasonableness stir up his reason; show him his error, admonish him. For if he listens, you will cure him, and there is no need for anger.

So if you are incensed, by all means, take control of this nasty situation and "show him his error." If, on the other hand, you would endanger your working relationship and consequently your emotional equilibrium, I interject my own studied suggestion: bite your tongue and plug your nose.

You may read Marcus Aurelius's self-directed advice on life in his MEDITATIONS. *He treats offensive odors in Chapter 5.28.*

-4-

Maintaining Sales Morale

Our sales force has lost morale as a result of a competitor. How can we inspire renewed confidence?

— The Management

There is no better ancient authority available than the great Roman general Julius Caesar, who lived in the first century BCE. While some praise and some blame this famous warlord, all agree that his charismatic ability to lead men was superb.

Julius Caesar knew the value of keeping information flowing, and he wrote constant accounts to explain why he had to engage in battles (and also to celebrate his exploits). As a result, we have a number of stories in which discouraged troops were rallied to a new vision and to victory, even against great odds.

Here is a perfect example. Led by their fierce King Ariovistus, Germans had been pushing across the Rhine into Gaul (modern-day France) and settling in Celtic territory. Caesar, according to his version, found it necessary to intervene with his troops in order to preserve the peace. He camped his men at a strategic city, waiting for provisions.

During this lull rumors began to circulate. Germans were huge. They were indomitable in battle. Their eyes were so keen that Romans couldn't look them directly in the face.

As this talk spread, a general panic took over. Some of the aristocratic commanders who were not experienced in warfare found excuses to leave; others who remained showed their fears on their faces. Comrades talked to each other of the impending danger. Men wrote wills. Even those who were experienced in combat were caught up in the general anxiety.

Caesar took control. He called a meeting of all commanders and reprimanded them for questioning his leadership. He noted that Ariovistus would probably not even be a problem because the terms the Romans offered him were so good (this of course was unfounded—but no matter). He said that they should trust in their own valor and abilities. He reminded them of former victories. Other tribes had conquered these very Germans in battle, he said—tribes that had not been able to withstand the Romans. When Ariovistus had been successful in the past, it was only because of trickery and surprise, not because of superiority in battle. This would not happen to the Romans. Supplies were soon forthcoming. Finally, he knew he could at least rely on one solid company, the Tenth Legion.

This speech did the trick. The Tenth Legion, feeling proud, rose to the occasion and assured him of its loyalty. Other legions apologized for questioning his command. Caesar led them immediately into battle, sooner than he had originally planned, in order to take advantage of their renewed morale. Although Ariovistus escaped in a little boat, Julius Caesar conquered the German army.

So to follow Caesar's example, get your middle managers together and give them a persuasive speech. Reassure them that you have control and broader vision than they do; offer examples of past successes; favor loyalty, shame cowardice, and welcome renewed vision. And then take immediate action. As Caesar well knew, the psychological factors were at least as important as actual battle skills. In your case, renewed morale is sure to bring your sales to new heights.

You may read Caesar's justifications for conquering Gaul and how he did it in his GALLIC WAR. This story is found in Book 1.

-5-
Overcoming Stage Fright

How can I overcome stage fright when I give a musical performance?

– Trembling Tremolo

You may take heart from the example of Nero, a first century CE Roman emperor. He too suffered from stage fright when he performed vocal music, yet he managed a successful performance career in spite of it.

Clearly, you enjoy music or you would never have raised the question. And music is a performing art. In recognition of this truth, you might take one of Nero's favorite Greek proverbs for your own motif: "Unheard melodies are never sweet."

Build your confidence by conscientious preparation, as Nero did. If you are a vocal performer, you might even try some of his techniques that did prove effective: lie down with a lead weight on your chest as you sing; restrict your body weight by both diet and enemas.

Once you begin a performance, don't let anything stop you. An earthquake occurred in Naples where Nero made his first appearance, and he continued undisturbed until the performance was over, as if nothing had happened.

Hire fans. Nero actually trained a number of young men in the effective techniques of rhythmic applause: the "Bees" hummed; the "Roof Tiles" clapped with curved hands to make a hollow sound; the "Bricks" clapped with flat hands.

Control the audience. Nero hired guards to keep people from leaving the theater, and rumor has it that women actually gave birth during his performances as a result!

Do not pass up any opportunity to perform. When Rome caught fire, for example, Nero caught the essence of the situation by donning his tragic costume and singing *The Sack of Ilium* from beginning to end. (No, he didn't fiddle.)

Carefully observe all rules in any competition you enter. Nero did. He was careful not to clear his throat or wipe away sweat; he addressed the judges deferentially, reminding them that the contest was in the hands of Fate but that as judges they would know how to "eliminate the factor of chance." Amazingly, Nero won every contest he ever entered!

Finally, maintain your artistic identity at all times. You might memorize Nero's famous words to be ready for your own last moments: "Dead! And so great an artist!"

You may read about Nero's winning artistic endeavors in Suetonius's Life of Nero.

-6-
Poetry as a Career?

How can I make a living by the pen?

– Penniless Poet

Unfortunately, it has never been easy to earn a livelihood by artistry of any sort. The Latin poet Juvenal in the early second century CE devoted one of his satires to this very problem.

Your basic options are to be independently wealthy or to obtain some other fluke of unforeseeable luck, such as a paying patron. Otherwise:

> Break your pen, poor wretch, . . . you that are composing lofty strains in a tiny garret, hoping to receive the poet's wreath! . . . The greedy rich have learned merely to admire and praise eloquence (just as children admire a peacock). In the meantime the years slip by which could have been spent sailing, soldiering, or farming, until your spirit grows weary and an eloquent but penniless old age curses itself.

Starving is no fun, and unless your belly is full, your poetry isn't likely to be very good anyway. How can we expect a modern writer, Juvenal asks, to compete with the ancient poets "when he must pawn his coat and the dinnerware . . . ?"

Of course, Juvenal himself continued to write. He confessed, "It is difficult *not* to write satire." Why not? Well, he had a whole list of pet peeves, and in these poetic satires he attacked people who in his opinion displayed hypocrisy, sycophancy, pomposity, avarice, corruption, and a litany of other things. (Not surprisingly, he devoted one whole satire to the worthlessness and decadence of women.) If he didn't make his fortune by the pen, he did seem to enjoy writing poetry, and he certainly gained his fame and a certain immortality by it. Taking this into consideration, I would suggest that you make your living in a more pragmatic manner, and if "the itch for writing and making a name holds you in its clutches and becomes an insanity," then by all means, continue to write on the side.

You may read Juvenal's jaded advice to poets, playwrights, historians, and teachers in SATIRE 7.

Health and Beauty

–7–

Mental State and Health

Does a patient's mental state affect the healing process?

– Remedial Reasoner

Absolutely. This principle is well attested by the best doctors in Greece in the Hippocratic Corpus, or body of medical writings that date from the fifth to the third centuries BCE. And a physician can have a great effect on the mental state of the patient.

For instance, the writer of the treatise *Precepts* suggests that a physician who loves humanity is the best sort, and he writes that some patients may even recover their health because they believe in their physician.

In order to keep a sick patient from giving up hope, a physician should recommend a specific regimen for the patient—this can counteract a despondency that might even lead to death. But when the physician properly takes charge, he can instill a confidence that may lead to restored health.

While fees are an important topic and should be agreed upon up front, they should not be brought up to the patient when he is in distress! It is far preferable in such cases to bear the ingratitude of those you preserve than to stipulate for payment while the patient is in danger.

Yes, your mental state will affect the outcome of a disease, and your doctor can have a great effect on your mental state. So be sure to choose a physician who is focused on the healing art and loves humanity more than money. Just don't get depressed (or ill) during your search for one who fits these qualifications.

You may read many commonsense recommendations on the artful practice of medicine in PRECEPTS, *a late addition to the* HIPPOCRATIC CORPUS.

–8–

Relieving Anxiety

How can I rid myself of anxious thoughts?

–Frightfully Fearful

Lucretius, a first century BCE Roman poet, wrote *On the Nature of the Universe* for this very reason, and he'll tell you what the world is made of as a bonus. Actually, he believed there was a link between baseless fears and lack of scientific understanding about the principles of nature. "For just as children tremble and fear everything in the dark, so even we at times dread in the light many things that are not a bit more fearsome than what children imagine, shuddering, will be upon them in the dark. This terror of mind . . . can only be eliminated by nature's aspect and law."

The world is made up of matter, he holds. And matter is made up of unseen atoms that are continuously in movement. To help you understand the principle, he offers a wonderful illustration: "For behold, whenever the sun's light and rays pour down across a dark room: you will see specks mixing in many manners, battling on in meetings and partings, as if in eternal strife." These atoms were set in motion long ago, and are actually moving in accord with unseen principles.

"Nature is . . . seen to do all things herself and of her own accord, without involvement of the gods." In short, you do not need to worry about any supernatural beings coming to get you, or about life in the hereafter.

Well, this only helps if your fears are groundless and if you're willing to accept the idea that everything boils down to matter. It evidently helped Lucretius with his anxieties, anyway. And I must say that I'm impressed (aren't you?) with this early theorizing on the nature of the universe.

Lucretius goes beyond technical atomic theory to extremely interesting speculations on life and good living in ON THE NATURE OF THE UNIVERSE. *These excerpts are from Book 2.*

–9–
Contraceptive Options

Every contraceptive method I've tried has a drawback, and I wonder if there is any alternative I've not yet considered.

– Exploring Options

Birth control is a very old idea, and much advice is available from antiquity. I'll offer you certain alternatives recorded by Soranus, a reputable Greek physician who practiced in Rome during the second century CE.

Dr. Soranus believed that anything with a styptic quality could be used before intercourse to prevent pregnancy, and he actually offered recipes. For instance: "Grind the inside of a fresh pomegranate peel with water and apply." A variation would be to take unripe oak apples, the inside of a pomegranate peel, and ginger. After shaping equal portions of the three ingredients into small balls, they were to be dried. Before intercourse, they could be inserted into the vagina.

A woman could block the cervix with a lock of fine wool, or smear it with a variety of ointments: old olive oil, honey, cedar resin, balsam tree juice, all with or without white lead. She was cautioned to follow these treatments with a drink of honey water, and to beware of very pungent concoctions that could cause ulcerations.

To answer your original question: yes, there are alternatives you've probably not until this moment considered. New (and very old) recipes and theories are interesting to contemplate, but I personally advise that you *not* experiment with any of them. In this case, please, rely on your own doctor's advice for modern contraceptive methods that will be safe and, whatever complaints you may have, much more effective than the ancient alternatives. After all, if these methods had been foolproof, you might not be here!

You may read Soranus's advice on contraception and other topics of relevance in his treatise on Gynaecology. *These comments were taken from Book 1.62.*

-10-
Complexion

How can I maintain my complexion?

– Fading Flower

Ovid, the great love advisor in the Roman empire during the first century BCE, asserts that cultivation, that great basis of civilization, implies tampering. For example, fleeces are most attractive when dyed crimson; beautiful figurines are carved from ivory (Romans did not suffer pangs over the possible extinction of species); palaces of marble are built over the black earth. In like manner, our complexions also will benefit from treatment.

Here is Ovid's solution in a poetic recipe:

> Strip the barley, which the Libyans have sent in ships, of its chaff and husks: this should amount to two pounds. Add an equal quantity of vetches, and the mixture should be made moist with ten eggs. When this has been dried in the airy breezes, bruise it with a rough mill-stone. Pound together the first horns that fall from the long-lived stag; of this, use the sixth part of a full pound. When now they have all been reduced to a fine powder, sift them in a hollow sieve. Add twelve bulbs of narcissus without the skin, which a strong right hand must bruise in a clean mortar of marble; add also two ounces of gum together with Etrurian spelt; to this let nine times as much more honey be added. Whoever will rub her face with such a mixture will shine more brightly than her mirror.

I will let you worry about accessing the ingredients, and even if you manage that, just to confuse things, the units of pounds and ounces were not exactly the same as ours. If this all seems too arduous a task, I would recommend a jaunt to your local cosmetics counter, where a current beauty advisor will be glad to offer you a substitute compound.

In the meantime, you may rest assured that even though the former users of this concoction are dead and gone, they died looking good.

You may be interested to read a number of other imaginative recommendations in Ovid's THE ART OF BEAUTY.

-11-
Party Dress

I'm attending a formal party next month and would like to wear something both classic and unique. Any suggestions?

– Thinking Retro

Fashions notoriously repeat themselves without apology, and each time they recur they are considered fresh and original. Think daringly beyond the sixties or seventies—back as far as the four hundreds BCE—and your requirements will be met.

The simple and graceful idea that I will offer is the dress inspired by Doric women of ancient Greece, who were reputed to wear clothes that allowed freedom of movement. The amazing fact about this *chiton*, as it was called, is that you do not need to cut or sew it anywhere, besides binding the edges—unless your fellow guests are very conservative and wouldn't appreciate an occasional side view of a leg.

Assuming that you are 5'5": take one piece of light, reversible, natural fabric 2 ⅓ yards *wide* (you will wrap it around your body this way), and 2 ¼ yards *long*. Using a contrasting fabric, sew a border around the entire piece of fabric, so that it looks the same from both sides. If desired, make a long tie belt from the same fabric as the edging.

Your sewing is finished. To complete the creation, you will only need a few accessories: the belt and two sturdy pins or brooches to hold the shoulders together. To drape this perfectly, you will probably need a little help from a friend. Align your hem at the ankles, wrapping the material around your body and allowing the fabric to meet at one side (there is enough extra width here to keep you fairly modest), and then pin at the shoulders, allowing the extra length of fabric to drape over in a large flap (see illustration). Cinch with a belt.

You will make fashion history at your party! Your statement will be not only classic, but unique.

Doric women engaged in much behavior that might seem odd—or progressive—by our standards. You may read about their lifestyles in Plutarch's LIFE OF LYCURGUS.

Food and Fun

-12-
Save or Spend?

Should I save for the future or spend now?

– Resourcefully Restricted

Enjoy life now! What good will money do you in your old age any-way—assuming you even reach old age? Or so advises Horace, the great Augustan poet of the first century BCE, in a number of his famous odes. For instance:

> "Fresh youth and beauty are speeding fast away behind
> us . . .
>> Not forever do the flowers of spring retain their
>> glory . . .
>> Why with planning for the future, weary your soul
>> unequal to the task? Why not rather quaff the
>> wine . . . ?"

Again:

> ". . . You are doomed to die whether you live always sad,
>> Or reclining in grassy nook take delight on holidays
>>> in some choice vintage of Falernian wine. . . .
>> Bid slaves bring here wines and perfumes
>>> and the too-brief blossoms of the lovely rose,
>>>> while Fortune and youth allow. . . ."

Of course, with the favored patronage Horace received from the emperor Augustus, he could afford both slaves and wine, and he actually had resources to provide for his old age. But Horace had "Plan B" in readiness, just in case his circumstances changed:

> "I praise [Fortune] while she stays,
>   but if she shakes her wings for flight,
> I renounce her gifts and wrap myself in my virtue,
>   and woo honest Poverty. . . ."

His most essential guideline was to be able to say each day, "*Vixi*"—"I lived."

Save or spend? Enjoy your life, whatever Fortune brings your way.

You may read Horace's measured admonitions to carpe diem *in his* ODES *Book I, 9 and 10; Book II, 3 and 11; and Book III, 29, among others.*

-13-
Resorts and Women

Where could I go to increase my chances of meeting available women?

– Sad and Lonely

While clever and manipulative suggestions are offered by the great love poet Ovid, I prefer to turn to the unassuming Pausanias, a second century CE travel guide for ancient Greece. Here is an observant, scholarly, religious man who does not strike one as a sophisticated seducer of women. Yet he evidently met with success in the small Greek seaside town of Patrae.

He offers two reasons for his love of this inspirational place: first, there was a sanctuary to Aphrodite, the Greek goddess of love, with a sacred grove by the sea, "a delightful place for idling in the summer." (He notes that there were also good rides, which he unfortunately neglects to describe.) Second, there were twice as many women there as men, and "if ever women belonged to Aphrodite, they do."

Patras, as it is now called, is a bustling city of 150,000 and reputedly has a lovely walkway along the quay. But even if it is not on your next vacation itinerary, you may still put to use the principles Pausanias mentioned. First, choose a place where women "idle," preferably at a sea resort where there are rides you can enjoy (parasailing?). Secondly, do a bit of statistical research on the ratio between women and men before making definitive plans for this potential spot (Caribbean cruises might be a good alternative). (Men: don't go to Alaska!)

The last ingredient is more difficult, since the worship of Aphrodite went out with the advent of Christianity. Nevertheless, one might assume that human nature would still incline women to love men, especially where men are scarce. Good luck in your search!

You may read more about this alluring place in Pausanias's GUIDE TO GREECE *7.21.*

-14-
Main Course: Ostrich

What entirely original dish could I serve to guests whom I would very much like to impress?

– Deliciously Daring

I'll bet your prospective guests have never tasted ostrich. Serving this gangly bird is an old art. Apicius, the ancient gourmand and sponsor of a culinary school, offers a recipe that ought to be as exquisite today as it was two thousand years ago, assuming that your bird is up to date.

While ostrich is rather expensive and hard to find, Apicius never let rarity or price determine his menu. He held that the effort and the money involved were a small price to pay for a dinner of delicacies. So—here is the rare recipe for your delectable dish:

Ostrich in Sauce

Cut the bird into serving size pieces and prepare it according to your own inclination (bake, boil, fry?), since this information is not included in the recipe.

The crucial point is to serve it in the following sauce:

- Place in a pot and bring to a boil:
  pepper, mint, cumin, leeks,
  celery seeds, dates, honey,
  vinegar, raisin wine, *liquamen*,
  and some oil.

- Thicken with *amulo* (cornstarch may be the best substitute).

- Pour over the ostrich pieces, and sprinkle with pepper.

- If you wish it more seasoned or tasty, add garlic.

What is *liquamen?* you may well wonder. This dubious product, widely used throughout the Roman world, was generally made of fish entrails and salt, a concoction that was then left in the sun for two or three months and stirred occasionally. The liquid that resulted was commonly used as a fishy flavoring. Use your imagination in finding a substitute for this one! And as the proportions of these savory ingredients are unfortunately not specified, I will leave them to your good taste.

Actually, I confess I experimented with this recipe on some ground emu that I found offered in a specialty grocery store. For lack of better, I used bouillon for the *liquamen* and threw in the other ingredients at will. It was surprisingly tasty.

At any rate, it will add a twist of excitement to the dinner, and you'll have a good conversation piece—whether your guests like it or not!

You may track down this and any number of other daring delicacies in Apicius's famous Roman Cookery, *Book 6.*

-15-
And Then Dessert

Any good ideas for dessert?

– Sweet Tooth

I will offer you a tidbit or two, again from Apicius, that great first century CE Roman connoisseur. He loved food so much, it is said, that when he had run through his fortune, he spent his last pennies on a fabulous feast. He topped off the meal with a concoction of poison, which helped him pass from this life to the next.

To his credit, before he ate that dangerous dessert, he included some healthier recipes for sweets in his cookbook. The portions are not explicit, and keep in mind that the word "pepper" was used very loosely in the Roman ambiance. Think of it as an opportunity for your originality to add flavor.

Spicy Sweet

- Crush pepper, nuts, honey, rue, and raisin wine.
- Cook with milk and flour.
- Thicken with a few eggs.
- Cover with honey, sprinkle [something good on top], and serve.

Sweet Fried Morsels

- Take a similar preparation and cook in hot water, so that you make a very hard paste of it.

- Then spread it out on a pan.

- When it has cooled, cut it up like sweets and fry the pieces in the best oil.

- Take them out, dip into honey, sprinkle with pepper, and serve.

Roman Toast?

- Break wheat bread into large morsels after the crust has been removed.

- Soak in milk, fry in oil, cover with honey, and serve.

These recipes have stood the test of time. May you enjoy your just desserts!

Indulge your culinary inclinations with these and other recipes, both common and exotic, in Apicius's ROMAN COOKERY. These are from Book 7.

-16-
Entertaining on a Budget

I love entertaining friends but at the moment my budget is limited. Can you give me any suggestions?

– Hesitant Host

Catullus, a clever Roman who lived in the century before Christ, found himself in a similar position. This did not hinder his hosting career. His solution was simple, as you will gather from the following poetic invitation to his friend Fabullus:

> You shall have a good dinner at my house, Fabullus,
>   in a few days, please the gods,
> If you bring with you a good dinner and plenty of it,
>   Not forgetting a pretty girl and wine and wit and all
>   kinds of laughter.
> If, I say, you bring all this, my charming friend,
>   You shall have a good dinner,
>   For the purse of your Catullus is full of
>   cobwebs. . . .

This ploy actually works. Some of my most memorable parties have depended on the guests bringing a contribution—and they have ended up thanking me! I highly recommend this old trick.

Catullus's entertaining love life is chronicled in his poems, which are easily available in a number of translations. This ingenious invitation can be found in Poem 13.

Lifestyles

-17-
Walk or Drive?

Why should I walk when I can drive?

– Sitting Pretty

Judging from the rise in traffic in cities throughout the country and the projected worries, this is not a bad question. Seneca, advisor to the emperor Nero in the first century CE, struggled briefly with the same issue.

Having elected to ride in a litter (Why not? He owned the slaves to carry him, and he was struggling with asthma), he complained that he was just as weary as if he had walked the same distance. He asked himself: why was he so tired? Well, because the exercise he did indulge in—being jolted in a litter—was more unnatural than the exercise of walking on foot, for which, as he points out, "nature gave us legs."

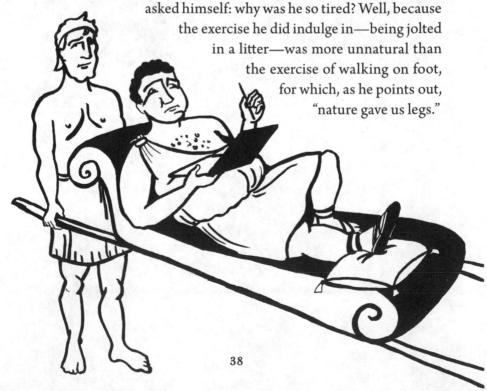

Never one to pass up an opportunity for moralizing, he theorized that "our luxuries have condemned us to weakness, and we have ceased to be able to do that which we have long declined to do."

Being naturally inclined to moralize, myself, I draw the conclusion that walking is better than riding. But I admit, on the other hand, to having driven several places today, all for very good reasons (yesterday, too). I own my car, I bought my gas, I paid my taxes. I didn't have the time to walk.

But my behind, I've just noticed, is stiff from sitting. I'm no better or worse than the ancient philosopher. He moralized, but he rode, too.

You may read Seneca's own account of this torturous journey in his MORAL EPISTLES 55.

-18-
Post Office

Is the US Postal Service unforgivably inefficient?
– Postponing Judgment

It is well known that the US Postal Service aspires to reflect the ideal set forth in antiquity, transmitted by the ancient historian Herodotus:

> There is nothing in the world which travels faster than these Persian couriers. . . . Nothing stops these couriers from covering their allotted stage in the quickest possible time—neither snow, rain, heat, nor darkness.

It is one thing to have an ideal, and it's another to live up to it. For comparison, I'd like to mention a story told by Josephus, the first century CE Jewish historian, where the fate of a good man turned on the speed of the post. General Petronius was under orders to force the Jews to worship a statue of the emperor Caligula that was to be erected for that purpose. Many other places under Roman rule had complied without comment, but by Jewish religious lights, this act would have constituted gross sacrilege. They explicitly preferred to die rather than commit this abominable act, and ten thousand of them rebelled by camping out, leaving their fields unsown, hoping to dissuade Petronius from carrying out his orders.

As a temporary compromise, the general wrote to Rome asking Caligula to reconsider and to make an exception for the Jews. In doing so, he knew that he was endangering his own life, and indeed, when Caligula received the letter, he wrote to Petronius threatening him with execution for insubordination—it was the principle of the thing. Fortunately,

> It happened that those who brought [Caligula's] epistle were tossed by a storm and were detained on the sea three months, while others that brought the news of Caligula's death had a good voyage.

In fact, Petronius received notice of Caligula's death twenty-seven days before he received his own bad news—which was now obsolete.

I think we can all agree that compared to the standards set during Roman times, our US Postal Service comes out looking pretty good, whether or not it matches the ideal of the ancient Persians. And if your mail comes late, maybe there's a cosmic reason for it.

You may read this striking story in detail in Josephus's WARS OF THE JEWS, Book 2, Chapter 10. Herodotus's comment about the Persian mail system can be found in THE HISTORIES, Book 8.

-19-
Yard Work

I'm sick of pulling weeds. How can I best avoid it and keep my yard decent at the same time?

– Grudging Grunging

Nothing easier! If, that is, you're asking Cato the Elder, whose opinion, I admit, is embarrassingly beyond politically incorrect. But he's long dead, and at the time he was proud to hold to his principles.

His advice was to buy slaves and train them to do the work. Cato was proud that he never overpaid for slaves, "because he was not looking for exquisite or handsome ones"—qualities that would increase their price but have no effect on their actual usefulness. He went so far as to boast that when slaves were too old to work, he would sell them rather than feed useless mouths.

Let's face it, slaves would solve your yard work problems, and when they outlived their usefulness, you could retrieve some of your investment.

I must modify Cato's advice by noting that Plutarch, Cato's biographer, takes issue with his attitude toward slavery, and devotes three rather long paragraphs to contemplating how slaves should be treated. (We must forgive him for not advocating complete eradication of the institution.) He states, "As for myself, I would not so much as sell my draught ox on the account of his age, much less for a small piece of money sell a poor old man and so chase him . . . out of the place where he has lived a long while, and also out of the manner of living he has been accustomed to. . . ."

Fortunately, slavery is one long-standing institution that, though once universally accepted, is now universally condemned. Since we cannot take Cato's advice literally, let's do some brainstorming to solve your problem. Consider hiring a gardener once a week for general maintenance. You needn't even feel any modern guilt, because you don't own the person—just a bit of time and exertion.

If you cannot afford this, consider yard work as a new business opportunity. Once you build up a clientele, you can hire someone to do your own yard work. Problem solved.

You may read in some detail about Cato the Elder's self-righteous manner of life in Plutarch's Life of Cato. *Or go straight to* De Agricultura (On Agriculture), *from which Plutarch derives much of his knowledge about Cato.*

-20-
Pipes

What is the best kind of pipe with which to supply my house with water?

– Ditchdigger

Apart from open conduits, the Roman architectural expert Vitruvius offers us two alternatives: lead and earthenware pipes. I'll describe for you the pros and cons he sets forth.

The more expensive alternative is lead pipes, which do have the advantage of durability. The drawbacks, however, are twofold: they are more difficult to repair, and the water flowing through them seems to carry a residue that is harmful to the body. In fact, lead workers suffer harmful effects, because when the lead is smelted, its fumes "take away all the virtues of the blood from their limbs," and the workers' complexions have a certain pallor. Vitruvius advises, "Therefore water ought by no means to be conducted in lead pipes, if we want to have it wholesome."

The less expensive alternative is the one Vitruvius favors: earthenware pipes. These pipes can be repaired easily by anyone, and the taste of the water is sweeter. He argues that "though our tables are loaded with silver vessels, everybody uses earthenware to preserve water's purity of taste."

With this knowledge accessible to us throughout the centuries, I'm wondering why it is I'm receiving constant public service warnings to let my water run several minutes so that I don't die of lead poisoning in my old house! Even if you choose to ignore Vitruvius and go with a more modern material like plastic (after all, Vitruvius didn't have access to the wonders of this modern, moldable medium), you might try purchasing an earthenware pitcher and test the waters, so to speak.

You may read more than you ever wanted to know about aqueducts, conduits, pipes, and water in Vitruvius's treatise ON ARCHITECTURE, Book 8.

-21-
Memory Techniques

How can I stop forgetting things?

– Researching Recollection

The techniques used in antiquity still sell on the self-help shelves of your local bookstore, where you will find the same methods for enhancing memory that were fully developed by the time of the Romans. Quintilian, a scholar from the late first century CE who wrote extensively on the skills of oratory, compiled the methods well known in his age.

To remember a list, associate items with landmarks in a familiar room—then as you review the room in your mind, you will be able to recall the list. Or you may connect symbols to anything you want to remember: a spear for a story about warfare, an anchor for a ship. To memorize a passage, write it out and study it from the pages on which it was written. Sometimes read a passage out loud, sometimes read it silently. Note the artistic structure of the piece as a whole and also its divisions, and assign a number of reasonable starting points.

After offering these traditional methods, Quintilian adds his personal opinion:

> If anyone asks me what is the one supreme method of memory, I shall reply, practice and industry. The most important thing is to learn much by heart and to think much and, if possible, to do this daily, since there is nothing that is more increased by practice or more impaired by neglect than memory.

If this seems difficult to swallow, it is softened by his suggestion to tackle only a little at a time, "in amounts not sufficient to create disgust," and modified by the common sense that "good health, sound digestion, and freedom from other preoccupations of mind contribute largely to the success [of memorization]."

And he advocates the string around the finger.

You may read Quintilian's memorable advice in Book 11.2 of THE INSTI-TUTIO ORATORIA (INSTITUTES OF ORATORY).

Human Relations

-22-
Nosy Neighbor

How can I tactfully tell a good friend when to mind his own business?

– Preferring Privacy

It would be a boring world if people minded their own business! This concept was immortalized by a clever second century BCE Roman playwright, Terence, in *The Self Tormentor*. The stage is set when Chremes, a rather nosy neighbor, asks Menedemus why he is unnecessarily toiling in the fields from dawn to dusk. Menedimus responds:

"Chremes, have you so much time to spare from your own affairs that you can attend to another man's with which you have no concern?"

Chremes retorts in Terence's most famous line: *Homo sum: humani nil a me alienum puto:* "I am a man: I consider no human matter beyond my scope of business."

In short, telling your friend to stop meddling will be an exercise in futility. Unfortunately, this does not solve your dilemma. Why not try sticking your own nose in his personal affairs?

To find out how effective Chremes's neighborly involvement really is, read Terence's THE SELF TORMENTOR.

-23-
Polite Vegetarian

How can I gracefully refuse meat when someone intends to lovingly prepare it for me?

– Polite Vegetarian

You are in good company, and your problem is not new. Apollonius of Tyana, a Greek philosopher and ascetic of the first century CE, was of the same vegetarian persuasion. In particular he refused to participate in any of the animal sacrifices that were typical throughout the ancient world of his time, and indeed, were a major source of meat in the marketplace. He followed the teachings of Pythagoras, and not only declined to eat meat, but did not drink wine, amass a fortune, or cut his hair. For a period of five years, he kept a vow of silence.

Apollonius was caught in the situation of being offered meat as a friendly gesture any number of times, but he was always able to deal with the situation with grace and goodwill, while never compromising his own decided principles. During one period of his life, he began a long journey to meet the king of India, and passed through many foreign lands on his way. As he was nearing Babylon, he was met by a satrap who threatened him with torture for trespassing and for not answering questions directly. But when Apollonius told him his name, he changed his tone.

Apollonius's reputation had preceded him. At once the satrap invited him to be an honored guest—he offered him gold, which Apollonius refused, and then excellent Babylonian wine which was normally provided only to the elite satraps, along with bacon and venison and other provisions for the road.

As soon as he had offered these gifts, he checked himself—because he remembered that he had heard that Apollonius neither drank wine nor ate meat. Apollonius simply suggested a substitute: "Well, you can offer me a lighter repast and give me bread and dried fruits." When the satrap also offered vegetables, Apollonius pointed out that "the wild herbs which grow free are nicer than those which are forced and artificial."

So here are two rather simple tips, based on the practice of Apollonius: let your convictions be made public ahead of time, since they run counter to the habits of the general population, and then help educate your hosts by telling them honestly what it is you do prefer. Apollonius's parting words to his host were, "My excellent fellow, don't keep your good manners to the end another time, but begin with them." Even the "barbaric" satrap understood.

You may read about Apollonius's holy and philosophic lifestyle, as well as many of his repartees with men of the world, in Philostratus's LIFE OF APOLLONIUS. This story is from Book 1.

-24-
Love Poetry

I am madly in love but, alas, am no poet. How can I express the depth of my emotion?

– Speechless Romeo

Quote Sappho. Sappho's words have stood the test of time in a way most writers can never even hope for. Given the dearth of women writers from the ancient world, she would be famous simply for her gender, but her skill and inspiration are what gave her acclaim. The philosopher Plato, for instance, called her the tenth Muse.

Writing in the seventh century BCE, she is among the poets credited with moving poetry from the epic genre to the personal. Although much of her poetry is left to us only in fragments (many bits have been retrieved from Egyptian mummies, including those of crocodiles!), you will find that her words suit your need. Even in translation, passion can hardly be better expressed. And fortunately, she was writing to other women, so you can use her words without changing gender, assuming your beloved is a woman too.

Here is a sampling of lovely quotations to fit any mood.

When you are overcome by love: *Now Eros shakes my soul, a wind on the mountain falling on the oaks.*

When you are lonely: *The moon has set, and the Pleiades; it is midnight, the time is going by, and I sleep alone.*

When you want to compliment her: *Well-favored is your form, and your eyes . . . honeyed, and love is spread over your fair face. . . . Aphrodite has honored you above all.*

When you want to set the stage for romance: *The stars about the fair moon in their turn hide their bright face when she at her full lights up all earth with silver.*

When you want to be truly intimate: *Stand face to face, friend . . . and unveil the grace in your eyes.*

When you are jealous: *. . . I have no sight, my ears ring, sweat pours down, and a trembling seizes all my body; I am paler than grass and seem in my madness little better than one dead.*

For once, I haven't got much to add.

You may find further Sapphic resources to buttress your amorous intentions in any collection of Sappho's works. There are many new translations readily available.

-25-
Prospective Wife

I've not had good luck with my previous marriages, but neither have I given up on the institution. What should I look for in a wife?

– Spouse Seeker

If satisfaction is any indication, we might take a look at Pliny the Younger's third marriage (second century CE) over which he waxed ecstatic. His charming wife's name was Calpurnia, and she was both very young and very smitten with him, if we can give Pliny credit for telling the truth. And he adored her!

We know a little about what made this marriage work because Pliny was an inveterate letter writer. In one addressed to his mother-in-law, he describes his happiness:

> She possesses an excellent understanding, together with consummate prudence, and gives the strongest testimony of the purity of her heart by her fondness of her husband. Her affection for me has given her a turn to books, and my compositions, which she takes a pleasure in reading and even memorizing, are continually in her hands. When I am pleading [a law case], she stations persons to inform her from time to time how I am heard, what applauses I receive, and what success attends the case. When at any time I recite my works, she conceals herself behind some curtain, and with secret rapture, enjoys my praises. She sings my verses to the lyre, with no other master but Love,

the best instructor, for her guide. . . . But what less could be expected from one who was trained by your hands, and formed by your instructions; who was early familiarized under your roof with all that is worthy and amiable. . . ? Accept therefore our united thanks. . . . Farewell.

In case you missed something, let me highlight the crucial points: you must already be established in a prominent and successful career. She should be young, chaste, and bright. Your marriage should be arranged by your future mother-in-law, who will have trained her daughter in what will please you. Your young wife should be willing to derive all her satisfaction from your career, and be willing to sit behind a screen, if necessary, while you receive public accolades.

So—the recipe for a successful marriage. Good luck on finding someone who will meet these requirements!

You may read many interesting details about Pliny the Younger's life, all told from his own viewpoint, of course. These excerpts are from his LETTERS, *Book 4.19.*

–26–
Mother's Influence

How important is the mother's role in the formation of her child's character?

– Maternally Minded

Let us consider Cornelia, who lived in the second century BCE, for a hint of an answer to this important question. While Cornelia was socially prominent simply because she was the wealthy daughter of the great Roman general Scipio Africanus, her fame was for being a great Roman mother. The ancient authors constantly referred to her as a mother to be emulated, and years after her death, a bronze statue was set up with the inscription: "Cornelia, Mother of the Gracchi."

Cornelia had twelve children, but in a fate not uncommon in her day, only three of them survived to adulthood: Sempronia, a daughter, and Tiberius and Gaius Gracchus. Despite the disappointments, she spent her energies on the children she did have. One telling incident associated with Cornelia took place when a wealthy Roman woman visiting her displayed her considerable jewels. Cornelia waited till her children returned and then said, "These are my jewels."

Cornelia hired the best tutors available for her children, including a Greek philosopher. She maintained an intellectual household in the Scipio family tradition, exposing her children to the most notable artists, musicians, politicians, and thinkers of the day. Quintilian, an ancient authority on rhetoric, noted three hundred years after her death: "We are told that the eloquence of the Gracchi owed much to their mother Cornelia, whose letters even today testify to the cultivation of her style."

Clearly, this avant-garde ambiance affected her children. Once reaching adulthood, each of her sons introduced progressive legislation to protect citizens with limited resources, and each was assassinated in turn for pushing the limits of Roman traditions and sensibilities.

After the first assassination, Cornelia's one extant letter records her complaints to her son Gaius Gracchus, fearing for his safety:

> I would take a solemn oath that apart from those who killed Tiberius Gracchus [the older son], no one has given me so much pain as you in this matter. . . . You should count it a sin to take any major step against my wishes, especially considering that I have only a little part of life left. . . .

It was too late. She had already raised her sons to think for themselves.

So in answer to your question, a mother's influence on her children is incalculable. Just be aware that, as in the case of Cornelia, they are learning the things you are truly teaching them, not necessarily the ones you have in mind.

You may read bits of Cornelia's life in the LIFE OF TIBERIUS GRACCHUS *and* LIFE OF GAIUS GRACCHUS *by Plutarch. Her extant letter, whose authenticity has sometimes been disputed, can be read in full in* WOMEN'S LIFE IN GREECE AND ROME *(Document #260). Quintilian's assessment is found in* INSTITUTES OF ORATORY *1.1.6.*

-27-
Division of Labor

My husband and I have disagreements on how household responsibilities should be divided. Any advice from the ancients?

–Haggard Housewife

Let us ask Xenophon, a prominent Greek from the fourth century BCE, who considered himself forward thinking and was quite liberal for his times. He held that "[Divinity] has bestowed memory and the power of attention upon both impartially, so that you cannot distinguish whether the female or the male has the larger portion of them." He says that a man and wife need "aid from one another, and the pair are of greater service to each other, when the one is able to do those things in which the other is deficient."

This sounds fair minded. But how is it that they complement each other? His answer here is traditional rather than provocative for his day, and he argues based on irrefutable nature: "The gods have plainly adapted the nature of the woman for works and duties within doors, and that of the man for works and duties without doors." To prove his point, he asserts that women have greater love for children and are therefore better adapted to care for them, while men have greater boldness and ability to guard the household.

Today, about 2,500 years later, the young man Ischomachus, whom Xenophon uses as his mouthpiece, appears insufferably self-righteous and condescending when speaking of his young wife and how he trained her to manage the household. I am afraid, to get back to your question, you will not receive much help from him in your attempt to divvy things up more fairly between you and your husband. Unless, that is, you take a hint from Xenophon's style of argument and can describe to your husband what it is that the gods have plainly adapted your nature to do, or not to do, as the case may be.

You may read Xenophon's ideas on the proper order and management of a household in his dialogue Oeconomicus. *Quotes are from 7.19–21.*

-28-
Neighbors' Squabbles

Two of our local citizens are involved in a petty squabble that is destroying the peace of our once tranquil neighborhood. How can we resolve this successfully?

– Aspiring Arbitrator

If we can compare your situation to the fourth century BCE Greek city-states that were chronically involved in petty wars, a solution can be offered. Isocrates, an aged orator who had tired of the strife, advocated a practical solution: to make war against a larger enemy, the great kingdom of Persia.

> We stand in need of some more durable plan of accommodation, which will forever put an end to our hostilities and unite us by the lasting ties of mutual affection and fidelity. . . . Never can there be a lasting peace established among the Greeks until they agree in making war against the Barbarians. It is then, that, animated by the same hopes, excited by common fears, having their resentment directed against the same object, and their affections confined within the bounds of their country, they will be cemented by the most indissoluble attachment.

Isocrates was proven correct when Alexander the Great a number of years later led the Greeks on that very mission. Peace was restored at home.

Uniting warring parties against a larger enemy is an infallible method for resolving disputes, and it works on every level, whether from petty sibling rivalry to strife between nations. In your situation, you might use this principle to involve your neighborhood in a fight against the city. Any issue will do: traffic, noise pollution, zoning, public schools, sewers, policing. Your squabblers are bound to see the common "enemy" as a greater threat than their next-door neighbor.

But let me add a word of caution. The Greeks certainly went right back to war with each other as soon as they had overcome their larger enemy. So to keep these neighborly hostilities from re-arising, avoid actually winning your cause.

You may read Isocrates's shrewd suggestions in his PANEGYRICUS.

Sociopolitical Issues

-29-

Striking Women

Can public demonstrations effectively affect legislation?

– Ardent Activist

Yes. There are several instances of this phenomenon in ancient Rome, but perhaps the most interesting was termed "the feminine secession" and took place in the second century BCE. Women left their homes, even coming in from the countryside, and brazenly accosted senators with their demands.

And what were they demanding? If we may rely on a speech reputedly given by Cato the Elder, the women said they wanted to

> . . . shine in gold and purple, and ride through the city in carriages on festal and ordinary days alike, as though in triumph for having defeated and repealed this law . . . that there may be no bounds to [their] expenses and [their] luxury.

Let me explain the context. During the extremities of the Second Punic War, a law was passed limiting women's luxuries so that resources could be directed toward defense of Rome. Twenty years later, the Romans had recovered their wealth, the men had recovered their privileges, and the women were still subject to the "Lex Oppia," as it was called. Women were asking for a return to tradition—and the legal issue really revolved around whether authority over women would be private and familial or public.

The interesting point is that the women

> ... could not be kept at home, either by advice or shame, nor even by the commands of their husbands. They beset every street, beseeching the men as they went down to the forum, that in the present flourishing state of the commonwealth, ... they would allow the women to have their former ornaments of dress restored.

When it appeared that they were close to winning the repeal of the law but that one crucial magistrate might veto the proposal, they besieged his doors and would not leave until he promised that he would not exercise his veto. The legislation passed.

So, yes, demonstrations can make a difference. It does help, though, to be demonstrating for a traditional right—or a traditional subjection, as the case may be.

You may read this striking story in Livy's ROME AND THE MEDITERRANEAN, *Book 34.*

-30-
Gays in Military

Should gays serve in the military?

–Ambivalent

The great second century CE biographer Plutarch would adamantly answer in the affirmative. While he was himself a happily married man, he looked back in admiration on the "Sacred Band"—a group of three hundred Greek soldiers who had a special relationship each with a comrade in arms. The group was termed "sacred," Plutarch suggests, based on Plato's assertion that a lover was a divine friend.

Plutarch believed that male lovers who serve together will be motivated to show courage in war rather than shame themselves before their partners and that they will readily rush into danger for the relief of one another. As a case in point, this Sacred Band died to the very man in support of each other rather than showing any hint of cowardice during the Battle of Chaeronea (338 BCE) fought between Greece and Philip of Macedon, the father of Alexander the Great. When Philip viewed the slain on the battlefield and understood that men of the Sacred Band were lying together, dead, he shed tears and said, "Perish any man who suspects that these men either did or suffered anything that was base."

Despite Philip's admiration for the fallen members of the Sacred Band, the fact that these valiants all died in one battle doesn't particularly convince me of their superiority as combatants. But if courage and not victory is the major consideration, one might argue that girlfriends and wives ought to engage in battle along with lovers and husbands to keep morale high. While Plutarch certainly didn't advocate that unorthodox idea, it may not be such a bad one. I say, everyone should be included.

Judge the merits of the matter for yourself. Read the story in Plutarch's LIFE OF PELOPIDAS.

-31-
Population Management

How can population growth be limited?

– Planning Planethood

This was not considered a pressing public question in antiquity because of short life expectancy and high infant mortality rates. However, on a private level there was a widely accepted and practiced method to control family size.

Let's consult a Greek living in Egypt near the time of Christ, Hilarion, who engaged in family planning. He wrote home to reassure and direct his wife: ". . . as soon as we receive wages I will send them to you. If—good luck to you!—if it is a male, let it live; if it is a female, expose it."

"Exposure" was an ancient euphemism for infanticide, although we know that some babies were collected by enterprising slave traders as investments in the future. Do you find this an unacceptable solution to population management? Let me stick up for this young man, whom we know of only from this one document.

He was not alone. In classical antiquity, until a father formally acknowledged a baby and thus welcomed her into the family, it would be perfectly legal and socially acceptable to expose the infant. (To do so after the acknowledgment would be shameful and socially objectionable.) In the case of an unwanted pregnancy, it was likely safer for the woman to have the baby than to take harmful drugs or endure other crude abortion methods. And the final selection could be based on more information: not until birth could one know what was in the package. It can be argued that our society's agreement to allow a pregnant woman the decision whether or not to carry the unborn to term is comparable, seeing that we now have technology that makes abortion procedures easier and safer for women.

I'm sorry. I cannot escape from my own cultural ethic enough to recommend the ancient solution along with Hilarion. If you are considering it, remember that it has been illegal since the Christian emperors outlawed it in the fourth century CE.

This translated document (Oxyrhynchus papyrus 744) may be read in fuller detail in WOMEN'S LIFE IN GREECE AND ROME *(Document #249). For a discussion on exposure in the classical world, start with "Child Exposure in the Roman Empire" by W. V. Harris in* THE JOURNAL OF ROMAN STUDIES, *84 (1994): 1–22.*

-32-
Animal Extinction

Why are rare animals still being killed, and what can be done about it?

– Endangered Species

Most ancient Romans appreciated exotic wildlife just as much as you do, but in their own way. They were entertained and titillated by seeing rare animals slaughtered in the arena. Because of the constant demand, some areas in the Roman empire became nearly depleted of certain species. For example, we find Cicero, governor of a Roman province in what is present day Turkey, responding to a friend's request for panthers to stock one of the spectacles:

> These [panthers] are exceedingly scarce. They take it unkindly that they should be the only creatures in my province for whom traps are set. So they have decided to leave my province, and have gone into [the neighboring province] Caria. However, the huntsmen are making diligent enquiry after their haunts . . . and whatever they find will certainly be yours.

If the panthers were complaining, Roman citizens were not. Nor was anybody ashamed of this. A great case in point is Augustus, the pivotal Roman emperor of the first centuries BCE and CE, who commemorated his life in the *Res Gestae* (Accomplishments of Augustus). This great brag sheet was to be inscribed on bronze tablets and set up at his mausoleum. As might be expected, he only included good and respectable items in this list.

Among other things, Augustus enumerated the great festivals he had provided for the Roman people: gladiatorial combats, athletic displays, and games. He then adds: "Twenty-six times, under my name or that of my sons and grandsons, I gave the people hunts of African beasts in the circus, in the open, or in the amphitheater: in them about 3,500 beasts were killed." Evidently, this fact enhanced his reputation as a beneficent emperor.

Why are rare animals still being killed? Because enough of the public still has a taste for it. What can be done about it? Since it was a nonissue for the Romans, we'll just have to extrapolate. I suggest you work at changing the public taste.

You may read all about Augustus's amazing accomplishments in his RES GESTAE. *Cicero's comments about the reluctant panthers can be found in* LETTERS TO FAMILY AND FRIENDS, 2.11.2.

-33-
Mandating History

Should history be a required course of study?
– Reconsidering Requisites

While Livy, a monumental Roman historian, did not address the issue of school curriculum, he did argue for the value and necessity of studying history. Among other things, he said:

> What chiefly makes the study of history wholesome and profitable is this, that you behold examples of all sorts of experience; from these you may choose for yourself and your country what to imitate; from these you may also choose what to avoid by observing what is rotten in its inception and rotten in its results.

In other words, the study of history could be considered an antidote for the fantastic fare on television filling youthful (and other) minds with diseased thoughts. It also may be considered an efficient broadener—students can find out about alternatives and enlarge their scope without experiencing certain damaging consequences.

And as he implies, knowledge of history can actually improve morals. Take for example one of Livy's first stories—the rape of the Vestal Virgin Rhea Silvia which led to the birth of Romulus and Remus and the foundation of that greatest of cities, Rome. One might draw the conclusion that rape is good because of its outcome. Or how about Romulus's murder of Remus in order to consolidate his own power? It was a very effective tactic, and he emerged unscathed. On second thought, this example thing, while educational, might backfire.

But one could argue that here is a prime moment to bring in the skills of critical thinking. And don't you think it's important simply to have heard about Romulus and Remus? I'll go with Livy: history should be required. Besides, I'm a history teacher. I need students. And I never get bored.

You may read Livy's comments on the nature of history as well as some rather exciting tales in the first book of his EARLY HISTORY OF ROME.

Government

-34-
Rueful Politician

In speeches I have advocated policies that, once implemented, have ultimately proved disastrous. How can I redeem myself?

– Rueful Politician

This is not a new problem and can easily be resolved. The great Greek orator of the fourth century BCE, Demosthenes, found himself in a similar position and devised a sophisticated system for saving face, which you can easily use yourself.

Blame the outcomes on larger causes. Demosthenes, who had persuaded Athens to fight Philip of Macedon and had then lost the battle, blamed it on factors beyond his control. First he blamed it on the gods—always a useful tactic. Then he moved to the earthly realm:

> Ask any man by what means Philip achieved most of his successes, and you will be told, by his army, and by his bribing and corrupting men in power. Well, your forces were not under my command or control, so I cannot be questioned for anything done in that department.

Demosthenes even turned the situation to his own favor by claiming he had actually won because he had not accepted bribes from Philip!

Shuck off responsibility by claiming your oratory wasn't, after all, that influential, using an ironical tone. "Of course the fate of Greece depended on whether I used this word or that, or waved my hand this way or that!"

Attack your accusers personally and claim that both they and their relatives are involved in odd and questionable cults. Claim to be a man of the people and compare yourself with adversaries who are elitist. Maintain your honesty and loyalty to the state until the bitter end: "And who is the deceiver of his country? Surely the man who does *not* say what he thinks?"

True, Demosthenes was eventually assassinated for having persisted on the losing side, but he never did lose his general popularity. Let us hope the latter for you and not the former.

You will certainly be persuaded that your career can be salvaged if you read On the Crown, *by Demosthenes, which also contains other useful political tips.*

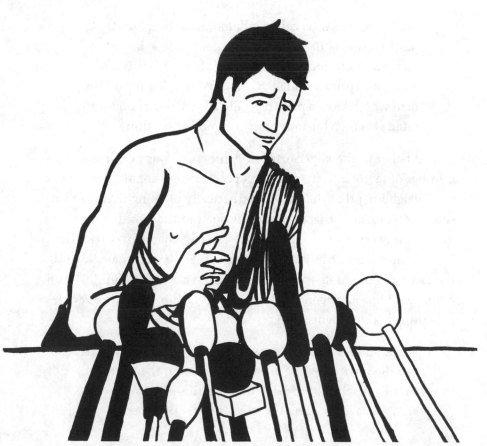

-35-
Ideal Government

Which type of government is best?

– Revolutionary Thinker

Pericles, the great statesman during Athens's period of glory in the fifth century BCE, speaks resoundingly, enthusiastically, and convincingly for democracy:

> Our government is called a democracy, because its administration is in the hands, not of the few, but of the many.... Here you will find in the same persons an interest in both private and in public affairs.... We regard the man who takes no part in public affairs, not as one who minds his own business, but as a good for nothing....

His belief in the superiority of democracy was confirmed by a number of factors: that Athenians practiced personal tolerance of their neighbors; that they lived aesthetically pleasing lives and had time for recreation; that the city was open to the world and to new ideas; that everyone was equal before the law; that men participated in the army voluntarily and were successful in battle; that above all, the city had pushed its way over land and sea and had built itself an empire. No one had been able to stop them. Who can blame Pericles for salting his comments with arrogance?

> We live under a form of government which does not emulate the institutions of our neighbors—on the contrary, we are ourselves a model rather than the imitators of others.... I say that our city is the educator of Greece.

These excerpts are taken from the funeral oration delivered by Pericles at the beginning of the Peloponnesian War, which was fought between the two most prominent Greek city-states of the day, Athens and Sparta. Ironically, it was the beginning of the downfall of Athens's political power.

And to agree wholeheartedly with Pericles, one must overlook the exclusion of women and the ownership of slaves in this idealized system, not to mention the democratic decision to make Socrates drink the hemlock just about thirty years later.

You may read about the Athenians' high opinions of themselves and their political system in Thucydides's HISTORY OF THE PELOPONNESIAN WAR, *Book 2.*

-36-

Laws without Loopholes

How can we set up a legal system without loopholes?

– Just Seeking Justice

This fair-minded question may be best addressed by Solon "the Wise," who wrote a code of laws for Athens in the early sixth century BCE.

Solon was not the first to attempt this. Previously Draco had written up a code that required capital punishment for crimes such as loafing or stealing vegetables, as well as for sacrilege and murder. Those "Draconian" laws, in the quip of one ancient commentator, were "written in blood, not in ink."

Solon took an opposite tack, in its way just as drastic. Instead of killing petty thieves, he offered a one-time, blanket forgiveness for all debts (imagine that!). This was only the most famous provision in his code, which reorganized the structure of government and also dictated how much finery a woman could wear. In his own poetry commemorating his achievements, he claimed: "I enacted laws for the noble and the vile alike, setting up a straight rule of justice for everybody."

Actually, Solon did not consider his laws perfect. Rather, he claimed to have merely given the Athenians "the best that they would accept." And as you can imagine, Solon made a lot of enemies. The wealthy resented him because they had lost resources; the poor resented him because he did not offer economic equality for all. To top it off, certain insiders took advantage of his plan and deliberately went into debt, making out like bandits when the law went into effect. As soon as the laws were hung in the public center, in fact, Solon vacated the city and didn't come back for ten years.

Solon has often been termed "Wise Lawgiver," but even he couldn't avoid loopholes. It may be, taking human nature into account, that we already have the best laws that we can accept.

You may read Solon's own view of his landmark legislation in Aristotle's Constitution of Athens *12 and 13, and other interesting details in Plutarch's* Life of Solon.

-37-
Just Judges

Who will render better verdicts, a judge who rigidly follows the letter of the law, or one who freely uses his discretionary powers in the cause of justice?

– The People

A quintessential example from antiquity is the emperor Claudius, who spent much of his energy in court as the supreme judge of the Roman Empire in the first century CE. Suetonius, his biographer, credits him with being "a most conscientious judge"—sitting in court even on his own birthday and on holidays, and always concerned to mete out justice to the people. Ironically, the very thing he was praised for also led to criticism, because in his desire to render justice, often he allowed his personal opinions and whims to influence his decisions.

There are many examples of his arbitrary methods: he sometimes decided in favor of whoever showed up to court, even without hearing the other side; one time, he wrote his verdict before hearing a case: "I decide in favor of those who have told the truth." If someone had committed a terribly heinous crime, Claudius might supersede the normal penalty and condemn the guilty party to the wild beasts.

His unpredictability led some lawyers to tiptoe around normally obvious items. When one time a witness did not appear at court as scheduled, the lawyer respectfully mentioned, "He is dead; I think the excuse is legitimate"; another, after thanking Claudius for allowing him to defend his client, respectfully added, "After all, this is the usual practice."

Any case that touched on Claudius personally was dealt with personally. Once he extended mercy to a man who had in the past given him a drink of water—a fact that had nothing to do with the case at hand. On the other hand, anyone who on the scantiest evidence was considered to be plotting against the life of the emperor was likely to be summarily executed.

Based on this evidence, I think we can assume that Claudius would have argued for discretionary powers. Based on this same evidence, much as I admire the intentions of Claudius, I'll take the rigid judge over well-meaning capriciousness in the realm of something as conservative as law.

You may read more anecdotes associated with Claudius and the law courts of Rome in Suetonius's LIFE OF CLAUDIUS.

-38-
Negotiation or War?

Why can't disagreements more often be resolved by negotiation instead of war?

– Fighting for Peace

That is exactly what Hannibal, the formidable Carthaginian general, asked Scipio, his Roman counterpart, before the crucial Battle of Zama in 202 BCE. The meeting itself was very unusual. Polybius, one of our major sources for this era, considers it a surprising idea that the two generals would actually talk things over before they rushed into battle. It must have been an amazing scene—two bristling armies facing each other, with the two generals riding out to meet in the intervening space, accompanied only by a translator.

In this famous meeting, Hannibal stated that he wished neither country had looked beyond its own territories so that all the past suffering could have been averted. "All that there remains for us to do is to try our best to avert the wrath of the gods, and to put an end to these feelings of obstinate hostility. I personally am ready to do this, because I have learned by actual experience that Fortune is the most fickle thing in the world. . . ." He proposed concessions that were apparently to the Romans' advantage.

Scipio explained why he was unwilling to accept this. If Hannibal, he said, had removed himself from Italy voluntarily and made the same offer years ago, it would likely have been accepted. Instead, Hannibal had wreaked havoc in Italy for fifteen years. In short, Hannibal wanted to negotiate a little too late in the game—now that he stood at a disadvantage. Scipio gave him the ultimatum: " . . . you must submit yourselves and your country to us unconditionally, or conquer us in the field."

The fighting alternative looked better to Hannibal than entrustment to Rome. (Who can blame him?) According to Polybius, in that decisive battle only fifteen hundred Romans died, compared with twenty thousand Carthaginians. The Carthaginians were now in the position they had fought to avoid.

In honor of Hannibal, Polybius quotes an old proverb: "A brave man meets one stronger than himself." And this is the answer to your question. When one side is in a stronger position, unselfish negotiation is unlikely to occur. I do not foresee world peace in the near future.

You may read about the battles between the incredible Hannibal and the dogged Romans in Polybius's THE RISE OF THE ROMAN EMPIRE. The meeting of generals is described in Book 15.

Morals and Ethics

-39-
The World Going Downhill?

Is the world going downhill?

– Hanging On

If the sermons I heard growing up were true, there is no question. We are all headed down that slippery slope, and fast—just look around. Disrespect, flippant immorality, violence, and disintegrating families are pandemic.

But what did the ancients think? Well, yes, they tended to agree. In fact, one impeccable authority, the great Greek poet Hesiod, observed similar phenomena in his own society. Writing approximately seven hundred years before the birth of Christ and three hundred before the pinnacle of Greek civilization, he told the story of the slide into the current deplorable state of affairs.

The first race, he said, was the golden race of mortal men who

> . . . lived like gods without sorrow of heart, remote and free from toil and grief. Miserable age did not rest on them. They made merry with feasting beyond the reach of all evils. . . . They had all good things, for the fruitful earth spontaneously bore fruit abundantly. . . . They dwelt in ease and peace . . .

He follows man's descent through the silver race, "less noble by far," who practiced violence against one another and refused to worship the gods. The third race, predictably, was bronze: "terrible and strong. They loved the lamentable works of War and deeds of violence." The fourth race was made of the Homeric "heroes" who were destroyed in war.

The fifth age was the age in which Hesiod found himself. "Would that I . . . either had died before or had been born afterwards. For now truly is a race of iron, and men never rest from labor and sorrow by day, or wretchedness by night." He concludes with a prophecy of further evils for future years: "Might will be right. . . ."

Which leads us, on the face of it, to conclude that the world has been going downhill for a very long time indeed. But—are we that much worse off? After all, Greece remains a wonderful travel destination—one I'd put on my list any day. Still, I'd watch my bags.

Hesiod's pessimistic views of life are contained in the Theogony *as well as* Works and Days, *from which these quotations are taken.*

-40-
Golden Mean

What is the secret to living the best sort of life?

– High Ideals

Really, it's not a secret. It was so much a part of ancient Greek wisdom that it was actually chiseled onto the temple of Apollo at Delphi: "Nothing in Excess."

If you want more detail, we should turn to that great Greek thinker and categorizer of the fourth century BCE, Aristotle. He wrote a book on ethics that, among other things, answers this important question. Like Apollo, he advises balance:

> We may feel fear, confidence, desire, anger, pity, pleasure and pain, either too much or too little, and in both cases improperly. But the characteristic property of virtue consists of knowing the proper time when, and the cases in which, and the persons towards whom, and the motive for which, and the manner in which—will constitute the mean and the excellence.

In other words, in each situation you must determine the middle path between the extremes of two vices: excess and deficiency.

Striving to reach this "golden mean" in daily life is worthwhile, I believe. I certainly aspire to do so, and most of the time (by moderate standards) I live a fine life. I highly recommend that you, too, take "Nothing in Excess" as your motto. And of course, remember to moderate your moderation.

Aristotle's proportional advice on the attainment of an excellent life is contained in his Nicomachean Ethics.

-41-
White Lies

Is it ever okay to tell white lies?

– Friendly Fibber

Not only are white lies permissible, according to Strabo, a first century geographer, but they are absolutely essential. In fact, calling on the "ancients" himself, he gives advice on how to tell lies most successfully.

Why would a morally upright Stoic like Strabo advocate elaboration, embellishment, and deception? Simply because children, women, and simple-minded men need to have their imaginations sparked. Religious fear, for instance, "cannot be aroused without myths and marvels." The generally uneducated populace will thus be encouraged to learn to live socially acceptable lives.

In traditional fashion Strabo calls on the highest possible authority from the ancient world, the epic poet Homer (author of the *Iliad* and *Odyssey*), to make his point. "As when some skillful man overlays gold upon silver," just so Homer added a mythical element to actual occurrences, giving flavor and adornment to his style. His hero Odysseus, for instance, "told many lies in the likeness of truth." They are still enchanting, three thousand years later.

And as for advice on effective embellishment: a person can "lie more plausibly if he will mix in some actual truth," so be sure to add a little fact to your fiction.

Judging from these comments, white lying is certainly a respectable practice, as long as the end result is both pleasing and noble. Personally, no matter how noble the cause, I find myself unable to tell even a little white lie. I assure you that every word I have written in this book is true.

You may read both factual and, we might surmise, fanciful descriptions and details of the Mediterranean world in Strabo's GEOGRAPHY. *His advice on fabricating is found in Book 1.2.*

-42-
Truth and Honey

How can I find the truth?

– Researching Reality

You can't. You can't, that is, if you accept the conclusions of Sextus Empiricus, who lived around 200 CE. This skeptic believed that even if truth did exist, it would be impossible to get at.

Sextus attempted to prove this by proposing the opposite to any given statement. For instance, if you said that honey is good because it tastes good, Sextus would counter that if a man puts it in his eyes, he'll believe it is bad. In short, whatever you might assert can be attacked from another angle.

Furthermore, if someone questions a "truth" you propose, you now need to prove your original proof—and if *that* proof is questioned, you need to prove yet another. You'll get stuck in a circle. "It is impossible to prove an infinite series, and so it is impossible also to get to know that something true exists."

If it's so hopeless, why bother? Just be grateful that Sextus can save you all that futile effort. In addition, recognizing the truth that you cannot find the truth can help you avoid the irritating habit of sounding doctrinaire and dogmatic.

On the other hand, we might follow his lead and make him prove his proof that nothing can be proved. Hopefully, he'd get stuck following his own tail. And as one of my friends pointed out, only a fool would put honey in his eyes. Now there's a truth.

Feel free to apply Sextus Empiricus's own principles of skepticism to his essay, OUTLINES OF PYRRHONISM.

Metaphysical

-43-
Omens

Are future events ever foretold by omens?

– Sign Reader

Let us consult two contemporary gentlemen of fifth-century Athens: the rationalist philosopher Anaxagoras, and the soothsayer Lampon.

Anaxagoras would say no. He believed that the mind " . . . has absolute power, and mixes with nothing, and orders all things, and passes through all things." With his famous mind he deduced, for instance, that the moon was simply a stone that derived its light from the sun—there was nothing magical about it. Elite men of Athens recognized him as a cutting-edge thinker, and he was the favorite tutor of the great Athenian statesman Pericles.

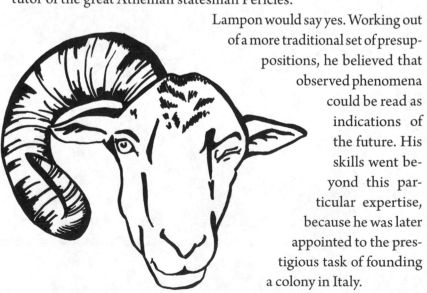

Lampon would say yes. Working out of a more traditional set of presuppositions, he believed that observed phenomena could be read as indications of the future. His skills went beyond this particular expertise, because he was later appointed to the prestigious task of founding a colony in Italy.

These two men went head to head in an interesting conflict between "superstition" and "reason," all because an unusual one-horned ram was born on Pericles's estate. When the phenomenon was made public, Lampon prophesied that Pericles would eventually consolidate rule of Athens and that it would be under him alone. Anaxagoras, who disbelieved this superstitious drivel, dissected the skull and noted that the brain was deformed, which had caused the bone to grow oddly.

Anaxagoras's view was favored by the enlightened sorts, but oddly enough, Pericles did eventually become the undisputed "Leader of the People." Plutarch, who recounts this incident 500 years later, comments editorially that "those who say that to discover the cause of a phenomenon disposes of its meaning fail to notice that the same reasoning which explains away divine portents would also dispense with the artificial symbols created by mankind."

Both were correct. I love answers like this, because they do not dismiss either side of life. In short, you may trust in scientific explanation and still pay attention to the omens which, if interpreted properly, may indeed foretell the future.

You may read the incident of the ram in Plutarch's LIFE OF PERICLES, *and more of Anaxagoras's beliefs in Plato's* APOLOGY *and* CRATYLUS.

-44-
Cults

**How can I know whether a new religious group
I'm thinking of joining is valid?**

– I'm a Believer

Celsus, a second century CE philosopher and member of the aristocratic class, gives us some guidelines in his famous attack on
Christianity. Celsus prided himself on both social standing and
reasoning ability, and objected not only to Christianity, but to a
plethora of other cults devoted to Mithra, Cybele, Sabazias, Hec-
ate—all of which engaged in "superstitious" activities. (We could
make a corresponding current list of ill-considered cults.)

Celsus's first objection centered on the type of people who joined
these varieties of religion. Most of the adherents were not only from
the lowest classes, but also had the lowest IQs or at least a high igno-
rance factor. Often they were women or slaves.

Beyond this self-evident negative, Celsus offers two criteria by
which any religion might be gauged: reason and tradition. "In adopt-
ing opinions we should follow reason, since he who assents to opinions without following this course is very liable to be deceived." State-
ments such as "Your faith will save you," or "Do not examine, just
believe!" are wrong-headed and ignorant.

As for tradition, in his open-minded way Celsus holds that "all men
consider their own laws much the best, and therefore it is not likely
that any other than a madman would make these things a subject

of ridicule." By way of example, although Celsus had no love for the Jews, he found their adherence to their own laws respectable, especially by comparison to the novelty of Christianity.

Voilà! You can now determine whether any religion you are considering is acceptable or not. But first, confirm that you are from the aristocratic classes, make sure you are highly educated, and double check to make sure you're not a woman!

You may read Celsus's dogmatic arguments against Christianity in CELSUS: ON THE TRUE DOCTRINE: A DISCOURSE AGAINST THE CHRISTIANS, *compiled from the early Christian Origen's* AGAINST CELSUS.

-45-
Curiosity

Can a person ever know too much?

– Curious Cat

It depends on what it is you're putting into your mind. This is a major theme of Apuleius's *Metamorphoses,* more commonly known as *The Golden Ass,* which he wrote in the second century CE. The story opens with a charmingly curious fellow, Lucius, who interrupts a fellow traveler's tale: "Excuse me, but I should like very much to be informed about what you are discussing—not because I mean to pry, but because I want to know everything in the world, or at least a good part of it."

This is Lucius's first step through a journey of misadventures. His initial mishap informs the rest of the story, for when he begins to explore the possibilities of magic, he is accidentally turned into an ass. The antidote, rose petals, is out of season and unobtainable. So he experiences his subsequent adventures frustrated in the body of this poor, observant ass. He learns more than he ever wanted to learn through sad experience. Stretched to utmost endurance, he suddenly encounters a revelation of the goddess Isis. Here is true knowledge, he finds, and as a side note he is given the means to be metamorphosed back into himself, now a true human.

Lucius turns his curiosity to the mysteries of Isis, which culminate in a death/life initiation experience. And from here he refuses to share his knowledge with the curious: "Behold, I have told you my experience, and yet what you hear can mean nothing to you. I shall therefore keep to the facts which can be declared to the profane without offense."

So to answer your original question: curiosity without boundaries is dangerous. It is better to wait for a revelation from the goddess. But I must mention one more detail: Lucius's earlier adventurers are a lot racier and beyond question, more fun to read. As long as I don't have to endure them myself, I'd take his misadventures over his religious revelations any day.

Apuleius's THE GOLDEN ASS *is one of my favorite readings ever. I highly recommend this wonderful, rollicking tale, which ranges from the profane to the deeply spiritual.*

-46-
Fortune-Telling

I need some informed counsel concerning a personal decision I must make. Can a fortune-teller be trusted to tell the truth?

– Fortune Seeker

Formerly, I would have recommended a trip to Delphi where Apollo transmitted advice and prophecy. He spoke through the Pythia— a common woman who, after ritual purification, sat upon "the tripod of truth." For over one thousand years this oracle was considered a most reliable source of informed insight and counsel throughout the ancient world.

There are many notable stories associated with the oracle, but perhaps the most famous concerns Croesus, the wealthy ruler of Lydia. He asked whether he should attack the Persian Empire, simultaneously donating much wealth to ensure favored consideration. The oracle replied that "if Croesus attacked the Persians, he would destroy a great empire." Croesus lost the war. He indignantly sent another question: was Apollo always in the habit of treating his benefactors in this manner? The god was unapologetic. He had spoken the truth— Croesus's great empire Lydia was taken over by the Persians.

Plutarch, the ancient biographer, was a priest at Delphi and wrote an essay arguing for the oracle's validity. There is nothing irrational about it, he said. Those who prophesy the future are simply better able to understand the past and predict the future. If Apollo seems ambiguous at times, he is simply encouraging humans to exercise their reason.

The ruins may still be visited at Delphi, but Apollo does not speak at that site anymore. The principles of future forecasting, however, remain the same. So to answer your question: believe your fortune-teller if he or she is speaking the true words of Apollo. If this is uncertain, simply make your own decision based on a rational consideration of causes and possible effects. Because if you had received an answer at Delphi, you would have had to use your head anyway.

You may read the fascinating story of Croesus and the Oracle in Herodotus's THE HISTORIES, BOOK 1, and Plutarch's explanations in his essay, THE E AT DELPHI.

-47-
Meditation and Time

How can I manage my time most effectively?

– Counting Seconds

I f you think about the concept of time properly, you will not have to worry about managing it. Allow me to introduce the momentous meditations of St. Augustine, that profound thinker of the fourth century CE, who may, I hope, offer you a timely new perspective.

Augustine's musings brought him back to early schoolboy days when he was taught that time consisted of the past, the present, and the future, a lesson he had in turn taught his own pupils. But he questioned this seemingly self-evident fact. How can one measure the present—by the past? Try it yourself. The present slips into the past and is no longer the present. And what about the future? It doesn't yet exist. "So it seems to me that time is nothing less than an extension. . . . Could it be an extension of the mind itself?" It appears that time is not something objective or measurable.

St. Augustine agrees that it's fine in everyday talk to speak of "past, present, and future, in our incorrect way." But having noted that commonsense assumptions are inadequate to truly explain things, Augustine moves beyond human observation for insight. That larger concept—a Supreme Being, always present, never future, never past, encompassing time completely, may provide resolution. The idea of the Supreme Being makes time irrelevant.

So in order to spend the duration of your life effectively, why not, like St. Augustine, contemplate the Supreme Being? If you cannot conceive of a God who envelops not only time itself but also eternity, you've just wasted a few minutes of your time and I leave you with your original question.

You may read St. Augustine's speculations on the nature of time in Book 11 of THE CONFESSIONS.

Ultimate
Questions

-48-
Later Life

Is there anything positive to look forward to in my later years of life?

– Loving Youth

It's nice to know you're not the first to ask this ageless question. The great Roman orator and thinker Cicero, who never hesitated to present a well-articulated opinion on any subject, left us a rather long treatise on the subject of old age. Among other things, he suggests:

> Enjoy the blessing of strength when you have it; when it is gone, don't wish it back—unless we are to think that young men should wish their childhood back, and those somewhat older, their youth! The course of life is fixed, and nature admits of its being run but in one way, and only once. . . . Each part of our life has a certain natural advantage which should be secured in its proper season.

In short, the pursuits of old age should merely be different, not nonexistent. Possible activities range from directing governments to writing and gardening, all of which require planning and engagement with the future. The key to continued joy in living is continued interest in life, because "No one is so old as to think that he may not live another year."

Do you lament diminishing physical ability as you age? Cicero can find a positive. "Bodily strength is wanting in old age—but bodily strength is not demanded from old men." Society will demand less of you, so you can do what you really want.

Are you frustrated by the thought that you may experience a weakened desire for physical pleasures as you age? This is actually a positive as well. "Nothing gives you uneasiness which you do not miss." Furthermore, "Imagine a man excited to the highest conceivable pitch of sensual pleasure. . . . Such a person, so long as he is under the influence of such excitation of the senses, will be unable to use either intellect, reason, or thought."

Let us therefore assume that it is preferable to rely on reason and maintain equanimity. Old age will allow you to do this, and you may look forward to it as a great positive. (But it was fun to imagine that "highest conceivable pitch of sensual pleasure," wasn't it!)

You may read Cicero's forward-thinking arguments in greater detail in DE SENECTUTE (ON OLD AGE).

-49-

Suicide an Option?

Is suicide ever justifiable?

– Option Opener

If you believe that experience best qualifies an authority, the first century CE Roman philosopher Seneca is certainly the man to answer this question. He not only presented a rationale for committing suicide, but he also did it.

Not that he advocated flippant suicide. After all, "there is pleasure in being in one's own company as long as possible, when a man has made himself worth enjoying." (We may suppose he considered himself worthwhile.) While he acknowledges that few people live to old age without some physical setbacks, simple pain is not reason enough: "Death under such circumstances is defeat."

As a Stoic philosopher, however, Seneca did believe that there was a time when suicide was the best alternative. He had defined that moment for himself: "If old age begins to shatter my mind, and to pull its various faculties to pieces, if it leaves me not life, but only the breath of life, I shall rush out of a house that is crumbling and tottering." He further contends, in a rather modern-sounding argument, "How much more cruel do you suppose it really is to have lost a portion of your life, than to have lost your right to end that life?"

As Seneca presents it, it's a matter of control. But at this point, I begin to have a doubt. Who can think straight in a moment so dire that one actually is considering this final solution?

In fact, when the moment came for Seneca, he did not make the closely defined and weighted theoretical decision he had envisioned. Instead, the emperor Nero, whom Seneca had tutored and advised for many years, ordered him to do it. But Seneca was ready for it, and the death scene recounted for us by the historian Tacitus seems almost choreographed. After he opened his veins (the fashionable way to exit at the time), and before he actually died, "summoning secretaries, he dictated a dissertation."

You may read Seneca's death scene in Tacitus's ANNALS OF IMPERIAL ROME, *Book 16, and his views on the proper moment for exercising ultimate control in his* MORAL EPISTLES *58.*

-50-
Gravestones

Can you give me some new ideas for an inscription on my gravestone?

—Arranging the Eventual

While the ideas I will offer are not exactly new, I congratulate you for thinking ahead! Already you're probably aware that your best chance for a sort of immortality two thousand years from now is an inscription in stone (barring prominence as a great general, king, or pope, plus access to a cooperative biographer).

What did otherwise obscure Roman individuals consider worthy of record? There were always career tracks. An illustrious aristocratic gentleman would record each step of his career—and athletes did the same:

> Apollonis. . . . Eight times he won in athletic games, but in the ninth boxing match he met his fated end. Play, laugh, passer-by, knowing that you too must die.

If a career doesn't encapsulate the essence of your life, you might turn instead to prescribed formulas (so standardized that the Romans often abbreviated the words with letters). For a woman:

> Here lies Amymone, wife of Marcus, most good and most beautiful, wool spinner, dutiful, modest, careful, chaste, stay-at-home.

If these generic adjectives unfortunately do not describe you either, a third tack would be to inspire enough passion to elicit a truly striking gravestone from your dearest:

> To Aurelia Vercella, my wife most sweet, who lived seventeen years, more or less. I was not, I was, I am not, I have no more desires. Anthimus, her husband.

All told, this is probably the most effective. Two thousand years later, I confess to a tiny tear for Aurelia.

You may also find other ideas for your tombstone in ROMAN CIVILIZATION: SELECTED READINGS: THE EMPIRE, *edited by Naphtali Lewis and Meyer Reinhold.*

-51-
Life after Death?

Is there life after death?

–Eternally Hopeful

No question about it. Immortality is one of those things about which you can be most certain, if we may believe in the Socrates whom Plato presents to us. Mind you, the arguments leading to this point of assurance are as slippery as debate, but they rest upon the best of foundations, a solid philosophical system.

Plato describes Socrates as offering arguments for the afterlife on the day that he cheerfully drank the hemlock. The discussion is filled with many entertaining conjectures. For instance, "The soul which has been polluted, and is impure at the time of her departure and is the companion and servant of the body always" is likely to remain attached to the body after death. This accounts for the fact that "certain ghostly apparitions of souls" have been seen "prowling about tombs and sepulchers." In fact, "they continue to wander until the desire which haunts them is satisfied and they are imprisoned in another body." And what sort of body are they likely to inhabit next? "Men who have followed after gluttony and wantonness and drunkenness, and have had no thought of avoiding them, [will] pass into asses and animals of that sort." (But reincarnation is another subject.)

According to Plato, Socrates based these seemingly superstitious guesses about immortality on his Theory of Forms, or Ideas. The system maintains that there are such things as absolutes—beauty, truth, and goodness, for instance—but that the absolutes themselves are intangible. Whatever we consider beautiful merely partakes of that absolute Idea of Beauty, which cannot be physically pinned down.

The soul corresponds to the unpinnable Ideas and the body corresponds to the many-varying manifestations of them. Since Ideas are absolute and never change, the soul may claim immortality. Since manifestations are temporary and vary endlessly, the body necessarily disintegrates.

I admit it, I simplified. If my crude arguments don't convince you, read Plato's *Phaedo* for yourself, in which more convolutions are added. In the meantime, the moral of the story is to live by abstemious philosophic principles, which will cultivate the immortal part of you and keep you from appearing after death as a ghost (or a donkey!) to some unfortunate bystander.

Read Plato's PHAEDO *to see if Socrates can persuade you of your own immortality.*

-52-
Universe

How far does the universe extend?

– Expanding Mind

I admire the broad-mindedness of your worldview—evident simply because you posed the question. Let us turn to Pliny the Elder for some advanced thoughts on the issue. Pliny is most famous for his dying moments during the eruption of Mt. Vesuvius in 79 CE, but he was also an illustrious Roman with a variety of accomplishments to his credit. His extant work, *Natural Histories*, is a compilation of scientific facts and theories of his day.

While many of Pliny's concepts now seem quaint, his thoughts are not always easy to dismiss, nor are they foolish. His answer to this question is a case in point. I suggest you contemplate it before you sleep at night. (Hopefully, it doesn't put you to sleep.) I quote:

> The world and whatever it is that we otherwise call the "heavens," . . . we must conceive to be a Deity, to be eternal, without bounds, neither created, nor subject at any time to destruction. To inquire what is beyond it is no concern of man, nor can the human mind form any conjecture respecting it. It is sacred, eternal, and without bounds, all in all; indeed, including everything in itself; finite, yet like what is infinite; the most certain of all things, yet like what is uncertain; externally and internally embracing all things in itself; it is the work of nature and itself constitutes nature.

Are there actual dimensions to the universe? Clearly, "billions and billions" would not satisfy Pliny:

> It is madness to harass the mind, as some have done, with attempts to measure the world, and to publish these attempts.... It is madness, perfect madness, to go out of this world and to search for what is beyond it, as if one who is ignorant of his own dimensions could ascertain the measure of anything else, or as if the human mind could see what the world itself cannot contain.

No matter that Pliny's perspective would be fairly unacceptable to today's confident scientific world. I say he has half a point.

You may read Pliny's intriguing descriptions of the universe in NATURAL HISTORIES, *Book 2. 1.*

Bibliography

Note: For the most part, I have used older translations that are in the public domain. Often there are many alternative translations available, including some that are more recent.

1.   Tacitus. *Germania*. Based on a translation by Sir William Peterson. Loeb Classical Library. Cambridge: Harvard University Press, 1914.

2.   Theophrastus. *The Characters of Theophrastus*. Trans. J. M. Edmonds. Loeb Classical Library. Cambridge: Harvard University Press, 1929.

3.   Marcus Aurelius. *The Thoughts of the Emperor M. Aurelius Antoninus*. Trans. George Long. London: George Bell and Sons, 1880.

4.   Julius Caesar. *The Gallic War*. Trans. Joseph Pearl. Great Neck, New York: Barron's Educational Series, 1962.

5.   Suetonius. "Life of Nero." *The Twelve Caesars*. Trans. Robert Graves. New York: Viking Penguin, 1957.

6.   Juvenal. "Satire VII." *Juvenal and Perseus*. Based on a translation by G. G. Ramsay. Loeb Classical Library. Cambridge: Harvard University Press, 1918.

7.   Hippocrates. "Precepts." *Hippocrates*. Based on a translation by John Redman Coxe, M. S. Philadelphia, 1846. Also consult the newer translation by W. H. S. Jones: *Hippocrates*, Vol. I. Loeb Classical Library. Cambridge: Harvard University Press, 1923.

8.   Lucretius. *De Rerum Natura*. Based on a translation by William Ellery Leonard. New York: E.P. Dutton, 1916.

9.   Soranus. *Gynecology*. Trans. Owsei Temkin. Baltimore: The Johns Hopkins University Press, 1956.

10.   Ovid. *The Art of Beauty* (*De Medicamine Faciei, or The Care of the Complexion*). Based on a translation by Henry T. Riley, B. A. London, 1877.

11.   Plutarch. "Life of Lycurgus." *Plutarch: Lives of the Noble Greeks.* Ed. Edmund Fuller. New York: Dell Publishing Company, 1959.

12.   Apicius. *De Re Coquinaria*. Based on a translation by Joseph Dommers Vehling. New York: Dover Publications, n.d.

13.   Apicius. *De Re Coquinaria*. See above, No. 12.

14.   Catullus. *Catullus, Tibullus, and Pervigilium Veneris*. Trans. F. W. Cornish. Loeb Classical Library. Cambridge: Harvard University Press, 1913.

15.   Horace. *The Odes and Epodes*. Trans. C. E. Bennett. Loeb Classical Library. Cambridge: Harvard University Press, 1918.

16.   Pausanias. *Guide to Greece*. Trans. Peter Levi. Volume I. New York: Viking Penguin, 1971.

17.   Seneca. *Moral Epistles*. Trans. Richard M. Gummere. Volume I. Loeb Classical Library. Cambridge: Harvard University Press, 1913.

18a. Josephus. "Wars of the Jews." *The Complete Works of Flavius Josephus*. Trans. William Whiston, A. M. Philadelphia: John E. Potter & Co., 1895.

18b. Herodotus. *The Histories*. Trans. Aubrey de Sélincourt. New York: Viking Penguin, 1954.

19.   Plutarch. "Life of Marcus Cato." *Plutarch: The Lives of the Noble Grecians and Romans*. Based on translation by John Dryden; revised by Arthur Hugh Clough. New York: Random House, n. d.

20.   Vitruvius. *On Architecture*. Based on a translation by M. H. Morgan. Cambridge: Harvard University Press, 1914.

21.   Quintilian. *The Institutio Oratoria*. Trans. H. E. Butler. Volume IV. Loeb Classical Library. Cambridge: Harvard University Press, 1922.

22a. Terence. *Terence*. Volume I. "The Self Tormentor." Trans. John Sargeaunt. London: William Heinemann, 1912.

22b. Terence. "The Self Tormentor." *The Comedies*. Trans. Betty Radice. New York: Viking Penguin, 1965.

23.   Philostratus. *The Life of Apollonius of Tyana*. Volume I. Loeb Classical Library. Cambridge: Harvard University Press, 1912.

24.   Sappho. *Sappho: Memoir, Text, Selected Renderings, and a Literal Translation*. Based on translation by Henry Thronton Wharton. London: Simpkin, Marshall, Hamilton, Kent & Col, 1885.

25.   Pliny the Younger. *The Letters of Pliny the Consul*. Based on a translation by William Melmoth. Boston: Greenough and Stebbins, 1809.

26a. Plutarch. "Life of Tiberius Gracchus" and "Life of Gaius." *Fall of the Roman Republic*. Trans. Rex Warner. New York: Viking Penguin, 1958.

26b. Quintilian. *The Institutio Oratoria*. Trans. H. E. Butler. Volume I. Loeb Classical Library. Cambridge: Harvard University Press, 1920.

26c. Document #260. In Lefkowitz, Mary R. and Maureen B. Fant. *Women's Life in Greece and Rome: A Source Book in Translation*. Second Edition. Baltimore: The Johns Hopkins University Press, 1992. © 1982, 1992 M. B. Fant and M. R. Lefkowitz. Reprinted with permission of Johns Hopkins University Press (print rights). © Bristol Classical Press, an imprint of Bloomsbury Publishing Plc. (electronic rights).

27.   Xenophon. "Oeconomicus." *Xenophon's Minor Works*. Trans. J. S. Watson. London: George Bell and Sons, 1891.

28.   Isocrates. "Panegyricus of Isocrates." *The Orations of Lysias and Isocrates*. Trans. John Gillies, LL.D. London: J. Murray and J. Bell, 1778.

29.   Livy. *History of Rome*. Based on a translation by Cyrus Edmonds. London: Henry G. Bohn. John Child and Son, Printers, Bungay, 1850.

30.   Plutarch. "Life of Pelopidas." *Plutarch: The Lives of the Noble Grecians and Romans*. Trans. John Dryden; revised by Arthur Hugh Clough. New York: Random House. No date.

31.   Hilarion. Oxyrhynchus Papyrus 744, Document #249. In Lefkowitz, Mary R., and Maureen B. Fant. *Women's Life in Greece and Rome: A Source Book in Translation*. Second Edition. Baltimore: The Johns Hopkins University Press, 1992. © 1982, 1992 M. B. Fant and M. R. Lefkowitz. Reprinted with permission of Johns Hopkins University Press (print rights). © Bristol Classical Press, an imprint of Bloomsbury Publishing Plc. (electronic rights).

32a.   Augustus. *The Deeds of the Divine Augustus (Res Gestae Divi Augusti)*. Trans. Thomas Bushnell, BSG, 1998. Available at http://classics.mit.edu/Augustus/deeds.html. © Thomas Bushnell, 1998.

32b.   Cicero. *The Letters of Marcus Tullius Cicero to his Familiars and Friends*. Based on translation by William Melmoth. Volume I. London: W. Green, 1817.

33.   Livy. "The History of Rome from its Foundation." *Livy with an English Translation*. Based on translation by B. O. Foster. Cambridge: Harvard University Press, 1919.

34.   Demosthenes. "On the Crown." *The Crown and Other Orations of Demosthenes*. Based on a translation by Charles Rann-Kennedy. New York: E. P. Dutton and Company, 1911.

35.   Thucydides. *History of the Peloponnesian War*. Based on a translation by Charles Forster Smith. Loeb Classical Library. Cambridge: Harvard University Press, 1919.

36a.   Aristotle. *The Constitution of Athens and Related Texts.* Trans. Kurt von Fritz and Ernst Kapp. New York: Hafner Publishing Company, 1950.

36b.   Plutarch. "Life of Solon." *The Rise and Fall of Athens: Nine Greek Lives by Plutarch.* Trans. Ian Scott-Kilvert. New York: Viking Penguin, 1960.

37.   Suetonius. "Life of Claudius." Based on translation by J. C. Rolfe. Loeb Classical Library. Cambridge: Harvard University Press, 1914.

38.   Polybius. *The Rise of the Roman Empire.* Based on a translation by Evelyn S. Shuckburg. London: Macmillan, 1889.

39.   Hesiod. "Works and Days." *Hesiod, The Homeric Hymns, and Homerica.* Based on translation by Hugh G. Evelyn-White. Loeb Classical Library. Cambridge: Harvard University Press, 1914.

40.   Sextus Empiricus. *Outlines of Pyrrhonism.* Trans. R. G. Bury. Vol. I. Loeb Classical Library. Cambridge: Harvard University Press, 1933.

41.   Strabo. *The Geography of Strabo.* Trans. Horace Leonard Jones. Loeb Classical Library. Cambridge: Harvard University Press, 1917.

42.   Aristotle. *The Nichomachean Ethics of Aristotle.* Based on a translation by R. W. Browne. London: George Bell and Sons, 1877.

43a.   Plutarch. "Life of Pericles." *The Rise and Fall of Athens: Nine Greek Lives by Plutarch.* Trans. Ian Scott-Kilvert. New York: Viking Penguin, 1960.

43b.   Plato. "Apology" and "Cratylus." *Collected Dialogues.* Princeton, New Jersey: Princeton University Press, 1961.

44.   Origen: *Against Celsus.* Books I and IV. Based on a translation by Frederick Crombie, 1885. A good presentation of Celsus's original work, compiled from Origen's quotations, is *Celsus: On the True Doctrine: A Discourse Against the Christians.* Trans. R. Joseph Hoffman. New York: Oxford University Press, 1987.

45.   Apuleius. *The Golden Ass.* Trans. Jack Lindsay. Bloomington and Indianapolis: Indiana University Press, 1960.

46a.   Herodotus. *The Histories.* Trans. Aubrey de Sélincourt. New York: Viking Penguin, 1954.

46b.   Plutarch. "The E at Delphi." *Moralia.* Trans. Frank Cole Babbitt. Vol. V. Loeb Classical Library. Cambridge: Harvard University Press, 1936.

47.   St. Augustine. *The Confessions.* Based on translations by J. G. Pilkington (1887) and E. B. Pusey (d. 1882).

48.   Cicero. *On Old Age (De Senectute): Cicero.* Based on a translation by E. S. Shuckburgh. London: Macmillan, 1903.

49.   Seneca. *Moral Epistles.* Trans. Richard M. Gummere. Vol. I. Loeb Classical Library. Cambridge: Harvard University Press, 1913.

50.   Lewis, Naphtali, and Meyer Reinhold, eds. *Roman Civilization: Selected Readings: The Empire.* Volume II. Third Edition. New York: Columbia University Press, ©1990.

51.   Plato. "Phaedo." *Dialogues of Plato.* Trans. Benjamin Jowett. New York: P. F. Collier and Son, 1900.

52.   Pliny the Elder. "Natural History." *The Natural History of Pliny.* Vol. I. Based on a translation by John Bostock and H. T. Riley. London: Henry G. Bohn, 1855.

Index

Ancient Ideas Made Accessible

Latin Proverbs
Wisdom from Ancient to Modern Times in Latin and English
Waldo E. Sweet

Book: iv + 277 pp. (2002) 6" x 6" Paperback, ISBN 978-0-86516-544-1
CD-ROM: (2000) ISBN 978-0-86516-502-1

A collection of 1,188 quotations in Latin and translated into English. Approximately 100 authors, ancient to contemporary, are represented, as well as quotations from the Bible, state and institutional mottoes, and legal phrases. Quotations indexed by subject, author, and ancient works cited. Also available electronically; visit http://www.ipodius.bolchazy.com.

Words & Ideas
William J. Dominik, editor

Student Text: xxvii + 281 pp., 81 black and white cartoons (2002) 6" x 9" Paperback, ISBN 978-0-86516-485-7
Answer Key: vi + 135 pp. (2006) 6" x 9" Paperback, ISBN 978-0-86516-637-0

Unlike most etymology textbooks, this one presents the words studied in the context of the ideas in which the words functioned. Instead of studying endless lists of word roots, suffixes, and prefixes in isolation, the words are enlivened by their social, literary, and cultural media.

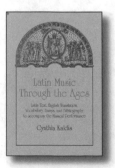

Latin Music Through the Ages
Cynthia Kaldis

Text: xii + 87 pp. (1991, Reprint 1999) 5½" x 8" Paperback
ISBN 978-0-86516-242-6
Audio CD: ISBN 978-0-86516-706-3

These arrangements come from all periods of music, from 12th-century Hildegard of Bingen to twentieth-century luminaries such as Pablo Casals and Francis Poulenc. The paperback book serves as the libretto for the performance on CD by the Lafayette Chamber Singers

BOLCHAZY-CARDUCCI PUBLISHERS, INC.
WWW.BOLCHAZY.COM

Cicero Made Accessible

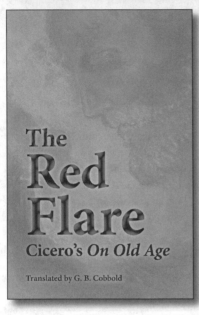

The Red Flare
Cicero's ON OLD AGE
Translated by G. B. Cobbold

xxvi + 92 pp. (2012) 6" x 9" Paperback
ISBN 978-0-86516-782-7

On Old Age is a gentle text. It has the capacity to soothe us when we read it as much as it must have soothed Cicero to write it. It pleases because of its great good sense and lack of sentimentality; because it deals so straightforwardly with a complicated topic that none of us can avoid; and in the end because it gives an answer that will satisfy most of its readers to the famous question "O death, where is thy sting? O grave, where is thy victory?" (I Corinthians xv.55).

Features

- Introduction to *On Old Age*

- Clear striking rendition

- Glossary of historical and mythical figures and places

- Two appendixes: Memorable Passages Quoted by Cicero in *On Old Age* and an annotated bibliography on Old Age in Literature.

G. B. Cobbold is the author of *Rome: Empire without End* (Wayside, 1995) and *Hellas* (Wayside, 1999). He is the translator of *Vergil's Aeneid: Hero • War • Humanity* (Bolchazy-Carducci Publishers, 2005). He holds a BA and MA from Cambridge University and has taught Classics in various secondary schools in the UK and USA—currently at Tabor Academy, Marion, Massachusetts.

BOLCHAZY-CARDUCCI PUBLISHERS, INC.
WWW.BOLCHAZY.COM